12 Steps To a Lighter Pack

Shaving Three or More Pounds From Your Pack

Steven Lowe

Copyright © 2013 by Steven Lowe

All rights reserved. Except for brief passages quoted in other media –radio, online reviews, newspaper and the like- no part of this book may be reproduced, stored in a retrieval system, or transmitted in any form by any means – electronic, mechanical, photographic (photocopying), recording, or otherwise – without prior written permission from the author.

Printed in the United States of America

ISBN-13: 978-1484187241

ISBN-10: 1484187245

Front cover photo by author
Back cover photo by author

Learn more information at: www.swlowe.com

For my father who has always believed in me and supported me in all my endeavors.

Steven Lowe

Acknowledgements

I want to thank my father for taking me camping for the first time all those years ago. This one is for you, Dad.

A special thanks to:
Martha Lowe and Elizabeth Grimes for their proofreading and editing my work.

A very special thanks to:
Andrea for her patience during this process and for putting up with me during all my backpacking adventures.
I promise I will be safe.

Steven Lowe

CONTENTS

Contents

Introduction 2

Step 1 Your Pack 6

Step 2 Luxury Items 8

Step 3 Food Choices...10

Step 4 Sleeping Bag..13

Step 5 Shelter..15

Step 6 Personal Kit 18

Step 7 Clothing Choices 23

Step 8 The Kitchen 26

Step 9 Fire Kit...30

Step 10 Water Purification......................................32

Step 11 Dual-Purpose Items 35

Step 12 Three Pile Process 38

Closing..44

About Steve 45

Appendix A...46

*"The journey of a thousand miles
begins with a single step"*

-Lao Tzu

Introduction

The journey to lightening the load on your back will also start with a single step. You may have already taken that initial step, and even if you have not taken an initial step, the 12 steps you are about to take will be a small part of an enlightening journey. A journey to get you closer to a lighter pack, for which your back and knees will thank you. I know mine thank me after every trip.

I have been camping with my family since before I can remember. When I graduated to backpacking I, like many of you, started out with a very heavy pack. I have done extensive research over the years, and tested many techniques, trying to lighten my pack as much as possible.

Because of this, I have turned into a Gram Weenie. In my next book, *Plan Right and Pack Light*, I tell that story as well as offer more tips on how to lighten your load. For now, let's just start with 12 simple steps that will help you lighten your load a few ounces at a time.

While writing my book Plan Right and Pack Light, I saw the twelve steps, that are listed here, emerge. I put a hold on the book and focused on these twelve steps to put it out as a quick E-book. As I was writing I noticed much more content than I initially thought, so I decided to concentrate on these 12 steps.

There is not one book, one piece of advice, or one class that will teach you all that you would need to know on how to lighten your pack. It takes research, experience on the trail, as well as trial and error to figure it all out; and I am still learning. I learn something on every trip I take, and I have been camping since I was knee-high to an acorn.

Using the following 12 steps, you can shave three or more pounds from your pack. This is possible, if you can shave an average of four ounces in each step. Don't trust me, trust the math.

There are 16 ounces in a pound. If you can shave four ounces in each of the twelve steps, you can cut 48 ounces from your pack – that's three pounds.

Life has a learning curve and so does backpacking. Each trip you take, each book you read, each person you meet on the trail will be a learning experience. You might learn something from folks you meet on the trail like a new trick to setting up your gear, or learn about a new snack. Every trip is an adventure. Embrace it. Have fun with it. Learn from it.

These twelve steps are not meant to be the *do-all, end-all* steps of how to lighten your load. Just remember that many of us live by the rule that *every ounce counts* and we weigh *every item* that goes into our pack and we also count every single ounce.

Please do not get caught up in thinking *"I can carry this; it doesn't weigh anything"*. Or *"it doesn't take up any space in my pack"*. I have heard these phrases and even said them myself over the years, and this is a habit that we must all break free from.

These phrases are myths, because basic science tells us that *everything* has mass, weighs something, and occupies space.

The steps you are about to take, are simply twelve little ideas I have picked up over the years that I have passed on to others that seem to have liked the ideas. Some of the information may be new to you and some, maybe not. However, I'm sure you will take something away from this that will help you lighten your load so you can achieve a lighter pack.

Keep track of your progress. If you are reading the electronic version of this book, you may want to use a pad to document your progress. However, if you have the paperback version, I have added an Appendix in the back of the book for you to take notes on your progress. So, let's get started.

Please e-mail me at steve@swlowe.com and let me know the results.

12 Steps To a Lighter Pack

Step 1
Your Pack

The easiest way to shave a few ounces from your pack is to shorten the cinch straps. Cinch straps are used to tighten up your backpack into a very tight unit once the pack is full.

The packs I have seen over the years seem to have the same issue –straps that are too long. The straps are longer than needed, to perform the function for which they are designed. It makes sense to shorten these straps to a length more suitable to the function. To do this we need to cut the straps.

I understand that this can be a stressful process, because of what you are about to do. You can mess up a very nice pack, if you cut too much. Be careful with this and take your time, but you can do this successfully.

If I can do it, so can you. You will need a knife or a pair of scissors and a lighter.

DO THIS AT YOUR OWN RISK!
DON'T CUT TOO MUCH!

Loosen up all of the cinch straps as much as possible. Fill your pack with whatever you can; we are simply trying to fill the pack to make it as big as possible. I recommend you use some blankets or pillows so you will get the actual shape of the pack. Make sure you fill the pack until you can't put anything else in.

Now, you will need to tighten the cinch straps to the point of where they are only slightly loose.

Do you notice how much length you have left? Cut it off except for an inch or two from the buckles, or to the length that makes you comfortable. Melt the ends with your lighter so there is no chance of the straps fraying.

The primary goal is to fill the pack, loosen the cinch straps to the point where the straps have no tension. Then measure an inch or so past the buckle and cut the excess off.

NOTE!!!

You can always cut additional length, but you can't add length.

I can't stress this enough… DO THIS AT YOUR OWN RISK! You can really mess up a nice pack if you measure too short.

The above is only a suggestion. I did this to my Osprey and I practiced the steps above many times before I even looked for my knife.

I even marked the strap with a marker at the length I thought would work and carried the pack on a trip as a test prior to cutting the strap. I recommend doing this before you cut the strap. Be careful here, folks. Take your time.

Step 2
Luxury Items

Everything in your pack needs to serve at least one purpose related to surviving. It would be best if they served TWO purposes, but I will get to that in Step 11.

In my opinion the items in your pack, if you want to start thinking like a Gram Weenie, should serve at least one function dedicated to at least one of the following five areas related to your survival on the trail:

- Keep you sheltered from the elements
- Keep you warm
- Feed you
- Make your water safe to drink
- Medical items

For example, a knife can be used to make shelter, and help with building a fire. A tent, hammock, or tarp will keep you sheltered. Use a pot to cook in, as well as boil water to make it safe to drink. Use duct tape to repair items as well as medical treatments.

Are you starting to get the idea now?

As a Gram Weenie, I try my best to stay away from any item that isn't related to those five areas, though I still slip from time to time. Because I want to document my trips, I take along my camera. I use the camera to make videos for my YouTube channel, and take pictures; for this reason, my camera is a necessity –in my mind. All other items not related to the five areas above could be considered luxury items.

Luxuries from home can really weigh you down if you're not careful. I like to take along stuff that will be fun to have on the trip, but it also means more weight. We call them luxury items because they are items that you *simply do not need*. They are fun items to have, and if you take too many of them, you will pay the price in weight.

You need to ask yourself *Do I really need my I-Pod or Pad? My favorite book? My portable radio? My deck of cards?*

I have one luxury item (other than my camera) that I like to take —a small radio. Sometimes we like to have music playing in the background while we sit around camp. I don't carry it on every trip, but it is in my gear closet and ready to go if I want it.

In the Three Pile process, I discuss later, you will learn how to cull items from your pack and the luxury items are usually the first to go. I have seen hikers take luxury items on many trips that never see the light of day.

Every Ounce Counts

Step 3
Food Choices

Food is awesome. Think about when people are on a date; they probably participate in some sort of activity like a movie or miniature golf. However, I will be willing to bet my favorite stove that there is a meal in there somewhere. It may be a dinner, or lunch, or even a picnic.

You might find food at weddings, funerals, political functions, or in the back of trucks during tailgate parties before a ball game.

We love to eat. We love flavor in our meals. The ambiance. The food. The conversation. It's all very good.

Food is everywhere. Not just any ole' food, but great tasting food.

The trail is no different and you should not have to eat bland food on the trail. Bland food is bad. I don't like to eat bland food at home and sure don't want to eat it while backpacking.

For me, dinner around the campfire is what I look forward to most on a trip. I look forward to kicking off my boots, putting on my Crocks and gettin' a fire going so we can eat around the campfire –now that's what I call *Fine Dining*.

I have gotten imaginative with my trail meals over the years and so can you. Just make sure that the meals you plan are light. A good place to go when planning meals for the trail is the grocery store. You can find some lightweight just-add-water type of foods that are quite tasty.

12 Steps To a Lighter Pack

However, if you have trouble figuring out what to select at a grocery store, there are many backpacking food companies out there. Mountain House, for instance, has great backpacking food. I have tried several of their meals but I keep going back to Spaghetti and Meat Sauce in the "Pro Pack".

The Pro Pack is vacuum-sealed which makes for a smaller package, which also means, it takes up less space. However, I have a tip on how to make that tight little package lighter, and even smaller.

But don't stop with Mountain House; there are many brands out there and some companies like Harmony House even sell bulk items like freeze-dried meat-substitute as well as dehydrated vegetables.

Google *"backpacking foods"* and you will get over two million links to click on that are related to dehydrated foods, how to dehydrate, and how to make your own lightweight foods.

Have fun with this. You will find all kinds of information. You will get ideas on some light-weight food and you will start eating better than you ever thought possible.

In my next book I get into more detail on light-weight foods to take but for now let's focus on the tip that I mentioned earlier, on how to make dehydrated meals even lighter and smaller.

Replace the original packaging

For my freeze-dried meals, I remove the contents from the original aluminum packaging and put it all in a freezer bag. I mark how much water to add on the bag with a permanent marker and seal it up. This resolves two issues.

- I can lay the bag flatter so it takes up less bulk in my food bag and, since I eat out of the freezer bag, I don't need a bowl.
- The freezer bag weighs less than the foil pack – remember... *every ounce counts*.

I understand that these foil packs are meant to be the bowl –Wow... I just had a *Caddyshack* flashback..... be the ball, Danny...... be the ball.

Anyhow, even though the freeze-dried meals have their own ball... I mean bowl, the plastic freezer bags are lighter.

Now, you might say, *"Aww, you're crazy to go through all that"* my reply is this:

Let's compare the foil pack to a plastic freezer bag. The results are as follows:

I didn't have a ProPack of the Spaghetti, but I did weigh a pack of Lasagna With Meat Sauce.

Full foil pack of food = 4 3/4oz

Full Freezer bag of food = 4 1/4oz

So you can see that using the qt. size freezer bag saved me 1/2oz. for one meal. On a four night trip with 4 meals you save two whole ounces.

Since *every ounce counts* and you have to pack out the trash, the plastic freezer bag is the lighter way to go.

Step 4
Sleeping Bag

Your sleeping bag will be one of the larger items, as well as one of the heavier items in your pack. I discuss something called the *Big Three* in my next book and your sleeping bag *is* one of the big three. Since your sleeping bag is a large and heavy item, this will be an easy step to shave some weight. However this step will not be a cheap one to take, if you are currently sleeping in a synthetic bag.

Without a doubt, synthetic bags will be heavier than their down counterpart. Down also offers two other areas of superiority.

They can be compacted more tightly than synthetic, which makes them smaller, thereby taking up less space in your pack and they will keep you warmer.

Your typical synthetic sleeping bag can weigh up to three or more pounds, depending on temperature rating and brand.

If you do end up going with down, you can spend quite a bit of money, as you will see in the bag comparison below. Moreover, like everything, down has mass, which means weight so be careful. The more down you have the more it will weigh, but on the other side of the coin, the warmer you will be.

A down bag will weigh less than a synthetic bag rated for the same temperature.

While writing this section, I wanted to compare weights of my synthetic bag to my down bag, but I couldn't figure out the temperature rating of the synthetic bag. My down bag is an REI Halo, rated for +25* (F), is a regular and weighs 2lbs.

However, I did find the following:

I found a synthetic *Big Agnes* rated for +15* (F) and a Down *Sierra Designs* rated for +13* (F) that were the same size –they were both listed as "Regular".

The Big Agnes weighs 3lbs 4oz (52 ounces) and costs $169.95 and the Sierra weighs 1lb 15oz. (31 ounces) and costs $499.95. The two bags are similar in rated temperature and you can see the difference in weight –you do the math. Moreover, since the Sierra is down, it will be more compactable than the Big Agnes.

Research your area's weather patterns, where you usually backpack, to determine what bag to purchase. It may also be a good idea to work with the sales representative at your local outfitter to get the best fit, and the right bag for your needs. You may need a -30* bag or a +25* bag depending your sleeping habits and body temperature.

Sure, I could get a down sleeping bag rated to -30* (F) but in the area where I backpack, the coldest temperature I have been in so far has been +15*(F) so I have a +25* (F) bag. Since I am very hot natured, and I wear very little in my bag, I stay warm enough in my +25* bag.

Step 5
Shelter

Your shelter is another one of those *Big Three* items that I mentioned in Step Four. Your shelter is a very important item to have in your pack, and since it is one of the larger items, this too will be an easy step to take.

Your trip can be very uncomfortable, to say the least, if you are not protected from the elements.

The primary purpose of a shelter is to protect you from the elements, and you might see three fundamental shelters on the trail –a tent, a tarp and a hammock.

If you're hiking the Appalachian Trail or another trail with man-made shelters along the way, you may not need to worry about packing a shelter on your trip.

Tents and Tarps

Tents are bulky, heavy, and you have to sleep on the ground, which can be rough on the backside. Also with a tent, you need to find a level area that is clear of roots, sticks, and rocks before you can even think about setting up.

You also have to sleep on the hard cold ground or carry padding as a thermal barrier to sleep on. Not to mention running the risk of getting wet if a rainstorm rolls in; so if the weather looks questionable, you will need to look for a higher than normal spot to pitch your tent.

I have used a tent on several occasions but I prefer to not carry around an eight-pound tent and sleep on the ground –my Kelty weighs a little over eight pounds. When

I do take a tent, it means I also have to take an air mattress or some sort of pad to sleep on. The forest floor can be rough on the back so you need something between you and the floor. Let's face it, all that extra stuff means extra weight. I also don't like to carry hardware for a shelter if I can avoid it.

Tarps are by far the lightest way to go, but the same cons for a tent, go for the tarp as well. You need a level area and you are on the ground. In addition, with a tarp, you don't have as much privacy as you would with a tent – depending on how you deploy the tarp.

Hammocks

I, along with most of my hiking compadres, sleep in hammocks when we're backpacking and let me tell you, we sleep comfortable and warm.

On this step, you will have to ask yourself: *"Do I really want to sleep on the hard, cold, lumpy ground or suspended in a cloud of comfort?"*

I'm a little bias here because I opt for the hammock. Imagine sleeping on a fluffy cloud. My hammock, under quilt, and rain fly weigh 3lbs 13 ¾oz. I sleep comfortable, warm, but more importantly, lighter.

My Kelty tent that I used to carry weighs more than double that weight. With my hammock, I don't carry tent poles or any kind of air mattress either –just me on a cloud.

After a long day of hiking, my hammock is the first thing I set up. Once I have it set up, I lie down for a few minutes to relax and rest my feet, back, and knees.

Ground dwellers (those that sleep in a tent) don't have this luxury.

When they lie down, they are on the hard ground. Even if they have an air mattress or foam pad. They still have to crawl into a hole in the side of their tent and lay down on the ground.

It is easier for me to get in and out of my hammock than it is to crawl in and out of a tent. Oh and I almost forgot about one other advantage –in my hammock I can rock myself to sleep. It swings with little effort and I am out like a light.

With a hammock, all you need are two trees about 25 feet apart and it doesn't matter whether or not you are on a hill.

But this is not a book on hammock camping. I want to talk about going light. A hammock is also quite a bit lighter than a tent. To compare, my Kelty two-man, four-season tent weighs a little over eight pounds. As I stated above, my hammock setup weighs 3lbs 13 ¾oz, so I saved four pounds in this step.

A hammock does not come with as much bulk either. I don't use stuff sacks, so I just push my hammock into the open areas and pockets of my pack and I am good to go.

Step 6
Personal Kit

Toothpaste

I spoke with my dental hygienist some time ago and she told me that on occasion, it is okay not to use toothpaste. Eeeeewwwwww.... Wait... let me finish.

It is more important that you brush the food from your teeth than using toothpaste. She did tell me, however, that your fellow backpackers would appreciate you using toothpaste.

The toothpaste is more for having fresh breath than anything else. Therefore, to prevent your hiking partners from offering you a mint every time you talk to them, take toothpaste with you. Let's face it, a little bit of toothpaste would weigh less than mints anyhow so it is a win-win.

A tube of toothpaste, however, can be a bulky item as well as heavy. Remember –*Every Ounce Counts*.

On previous trips, I have taken a travel size tube of toothpaste, but since then I have started taking an alternative version of toothpaste, which I will get to in a moment.

While writing this section, I weighed a half-full "travel-size" tube of toothpaste that I normally would have taken and it weighed 3 1/8 oz.

I would carry the same tube for many trips and it was taking a long time to go through the tube. Why was I taking the same weight each time I hit the trail?

Some time ago, I ran across this tip on YouTube and have used it since the first time I found it.

12 Steps To a Lighter Pack

I call them toothpaste pods.

Here is what you will need to make your own pods:
- Straws
- Lighter
- Scissors
- Paper towels
- Needle-nose pliers
- Your favorite brand of toothpaste

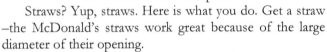

Straws? Yup, straws. Here is what you do. Get a straw —the McDonald's straws work great because of the large diameter of their opening.

Squeeze a small portion of toothpaste into one end of the straw. Keep in mind that you are making single use items here so you only need enough for one session of tooth brushing.

Wipe the excess toothpaste from around the exterior of the straw. Take your pliers and pinch the straw tight leaving about an eighth of an inch, and again, wipe the excess toothpaste from the straw. Take your lighter and melt the straw all the way to the pliers. It may take some practice getting the plastic to melt enough to seal the end.

Use your scissors to cut the straw on the other end leaving enough room to melt the end, and repeat the melting process.

Make as many as you will need for your trip and unless you skip a day, you will have a lot less weight on your last day when you hike out.

While writing this section, I made five pods out of one McDonalds straw. It took two pods to register and the two pods weighed 1/8oz. All five pods weigh 1/4 of an ounce therefore, I saved 2 7\8oz from the original tube I would have taken. Almost three whole ounces.

Every Ounce Counts.

Since one pod didn't register, but two pods registered 1/8 ounce, I switched to grams.

Some of the individual pods weighed two grams and some didn't register at all, but all five pods weighed five grams. So, they averaged about a gram each.

Depending on how large you make your pods, you should still have less than an ounce of toothpaste for a trip lasting several nights.

Hopefully, you can see the benefit of the pods verses a big tube of toothpaste. They are quite a bit lighter.

Toothbrush

Now that you have a lighter way to carry your toothpaste, what about the toothbrush? That is a great question and I am so glad you asked. Check this out.

I have carried a "travel-toothbrush" on past trips and it comes in two pieces. When being used, the two pieces fit together to make a long brush, but for traveling, one end fits into the other end. I threw out the case and only take the half that I really need. I can't find it since my last trip so I can't weigh it, so I guess I need to make another one out of a normal toothbrush.

If you want to take a normal toothbrush and make it lighter, simply cut it in half. This toothbrush weighs 3/8oz (15 grams)

Cut it in half and you have a shorter piece and it weighs half as much. Because my scale is not detailed in ounces, and even though I cut off more than half, each piece weighs 1/4 oz. but in grams the handle weighs 8 grams and the brush weighs 6 grams which means I removed a gram of material using the hack saw.

Since Gram Weenies count everything in grams, we can get a more specific amount of weight. Remember the pods above, I had to switch to grams to get one of the pods to register. Same goes for the toothbrush as well. So cut that toothbrush in half and you can save a little bit of weight.

Toilet Paper

Toilet Paper is also an area where you can shave a tiny bit of weight. That little cardboard roll in the middle of the TP is dead weight. It serves no practical purpose.

I weighed one, it only weighed 1/8 oz, but seven more of these and you have a whole ounce. Okay I know I am really pushing this Gram Weenie thing to the brink, but this is how we, or maybe it's just me, this is how I actually think as a Gram Weenie. I think about every ounce I carry.

This little piece of cardboard is dead weight, unless of course, you use all your toilet paper and end up using this cardboard roll to start a fire. In which case –GREAT JOB! This item turned into a dual-purpose item. Read Step 11 for more details on dual-purpose items.

But if you don't use all the toilet paper you have to carry around all that extra weight. Do you think I'm crazy yet, or are you starting to think like a Gram Weenie?

Try the Coleman brand biodegradable TP because it has no cardboard insert. It also seems to be more durable than regular TP.

On some trips, I have taken my home brand of *Charmin Ultra*, because let's face it; the trail is hard enough as it is; you don't need cheap toilet paper. Take the soft stuff if you can.

My Charmin is great here at home, but on the trail it tends to break down rather quickly getting knocked around in the pack, but the Coleman brand is still soft on the ole' tushy but tough enough to withstand the abuse of getting beaten up in the pack.

Step 7
Clothing Choices

In Step 5, I discussed protection from the elements using a shelter. However, now I want to go over protection from the elements using the clothes on your back.

Your best bet would be to stick with all synthetic materials. Stay away from cotton. There is a popular phrase among experienced backpackers –*Cotton Kills*. Here's why:

To keep this section short, I will spare you the scientific principles of evaporation and the different ways we lose body heat while backpacking.

The gist is, cotton holds more water, and holds the water longer than synthetic materials like polyester and nylon. Therefore, when cotton is wet, it loses its insulating value, unlike wool, which will retain its insulating value even when wet. So if you want to wear natural material, wear wool.

Basically, when water evaporates, the surface that holds the water cools down. Therefore, if you are in wet clothes, you will cool off faster than if you were in dry clothes. If this happens, you could slip into a dangerous area called hypothermia if you are not careful.

Simply put, hypothermia is when your body's core temperature is much lower than normal. A body's core temperature needs to drop only a few degrees to be considered hypothermic.

Wikipedia.org explains Hypothermia this way:

"Hypothermia is a condition in which core temperature drops below the required temperature for normal metabolism and body functions which is defined as 35.0 °C (95.0 °F).
Body temperature is usually maintained near a constant level of 36.5–37.5 °C (98–100 °F) through biologic homeostasis or thermoregulation. If exposed to cold and the internal mechanisms are unable to replenish the heat that is being lost, a drop in core temperature occurs. As body temperature decreases, characteristic symptoms occur such as shivering and mental confusion."

Therefore, you can see the danger in getting too cold. This can happen if you get wet while wearing cotton. So try not to get rained on, fall into the creek, or sweat too much if you are wearing cotton.

Your best bet is to wear synthetic material. You will not find any cotton in my pack other than a few bandannas. I stick to the synthetics unless it's my down vest, coat, and sleeping bag.

If you have a polyester shirt, wash it with a cotton shirt and notice how much they each weigh before the wash and after you take them out of the washing machine.

Now let them both air dry by hanging them on a hanger or the shower rod in the bathroom. Check both shirts every half hour to see how long each shirt takes to dry.

You will find that the cotton shirt weighs a lot more than the polyester shirt out of the washing machine, and the cotton shirt will take much longer to dry than the polyester shirt.

So, if your checkbook will allow, shop around and go with all synthetic clothes. They may be a bit more expensive, but they dry faster, are much lighter, and will keep you warmer while out on the trail.

Step 8
The Kitchen

DIY Stoves are another way to lighten your load. Most of the DIY stoves I have seen are made out of cat food containers, soda cans, and aluminum beer bottles like the one I have –Budweiser and Bud Light used to come in aluminum bottles. I have even seen some made out of Redbull cans.

You will need to take along a container to keep your fuel in that will not leak, but these stoves are wicked light. I have tried them, and on the trips during the warmer months, they work great. During the colder months, however, you have to keep the fuel with you in your sleeping bag at night or find some way to keep the fuel warm.

On a recent March trip up Springer Mountain, I forgot about keeping my fuel warm, and the next morning, I had to put the fuel bottle in my coat and walk around a while. Sure, this gave me some time to make a video and take some pictures, but it also prolonged "Coffee-O-Clock".

I like my coffee soon after I wake up and that morning I was not a happy camper –pun intended. I am hard to get along with in the morning until I have my coffee.

Speaking of coffee, your coffee cup is another area you might be able to shave a few ounces. This REI cup used to be my cup of choice.

I have used this cup on more trips than I can remember and I love it. On the other side of the cup, it is marked every two ounces; so I was able to use it to measure out my water for the dehydrated meals. This cup is dual-walled insulated –if that's a word, and fairly light. It weighs 5 ¼ ounces.

But I figured I could find a way to go lighter so I made my own cup out of a small plastic peanut butter jar wrapped with Reflectix. This cup weighed an ounce and a

half. It too was light, kept my coffee warm long enough for me to drink it, and I marked the cup with one cup and two cup markings so I could use it to measure water.

The problem with this cup is when I "tested from home" (which I will cover in my next book) the boiling hot water melted the cup enough to mess up my graduated markings on the back. This forced me to work with my dehydrated meals a bit differently. I had to work with the amount of water needed to rehydrate my meals.

Both of the cups above worked great. They were both light, they both kept my coffee warm long enough for me to drink it but, once the coffee was gone each morning; I had to carry the weight of the empty cup to the next campsite.

In addition, at the end of the trip, I had to carry out the dead weight of an empty plastic cup. I call it dead weight, because, on the last day, I am finished with this item for the rest of the trip and did not use it again so it is dead weight.

This forced me to keep thinking on how to go even lighter and then it hit me at a convenience store one morning. I stopped at the QT, here in Atlanta, one morning and got a cup of coffee. The coffee was in a cardboard cup and once I was finished with my coffee I simply threw the cup away at my next stop.

Hmmmm….. How can I use this little event to make my pack lighter? This is what I do. I am constantly thinking about my next trip and how I can lighten my pack.

On my next trip to the local grocery store, I saw something that I could use to replace my coffee cup.

They are made out of cardboard so they are light, insulated, (they are wrapped in an extra layer of cardboard) and they keep my coffee warm long enough for me to drink it.

Three cups, for a standard little weekend trip, weigh 2 3/8 ounces which is less than the REI cup, but more than the DIY cup. These cups meet all my needs.

This works for me because of two primary reasons:
- Each cup is individually lighter
- They are dual purpose items

Dual purpose in that on the mornings, after I drink my coffee, I save the cup in my trash bag and carry it to the next stop. I now have some cardboard to help with the fire starting. Or, the mornings we drink coffee and have a fire, I can simply burn the cup that morning and not worry about carrying it to the next stop.

On the last morning of the trip, either I burn the last cup in a small fire, or I carry out an item that only weighs 3/4 of an ounce.

This lightens my load because I normally would have a reusable cup that I would have to carry out. Remember the DIY cup weighs 1 ½ ounce and the REI cup weighs 5 ¼ ounces.

Now, I have *nothing* to carry out.

Oh, and one more thing, I also don't have to wash the cardboard cups like I would with a plastic cup; which also means I don't have to take any dish washing soap relieving myself of that weight as well.

Another quick tip is to carry salt and pepper packets instead of a plastic salt and pepper container. They are free at most fast food restaurants, if you buy some food.

As you eat out, collect a few of these and you will end up with a cache of salt and pepper to add to your gear closet. These can also be burned in a fire because the packets are made of paper so you are not hurting the environment —something else to think about.

Step 9
Fire Kit

Just as sure as the sun sets in the west, so your fire kit is the smallest kit in your bag —or at least it should be. And likewise, this will be the shortest step in the process.

During my many years of car-camping, we would take whole grills, piles of wood, lighter fluid and bags of charcoal to get a good fire going. I have used some of the pre-made *fire sticks*; I have even taken my own that I made out of cotton balls and wax, but it usually all boils down to a simple little item —a disposable lighter.

I have not used the fancy DIY fire starters in a long time, but I have always taken a disposable lighter, sometimes two. But now, all I take is a little disposable lighter that I gutted and is now packed with jute twine. The twine weight replaces the hardware and gas so this item is a wash as far as weight is concerned. If you know how to build a good fire you don't really need to carry anything other than a lighter. In my next book I will spend a lot more time on how to build a fire correctly, or at least in a way that has suited me for years, but all you need is a small disposable lighter.

To build a fire right, all you need is a single spark and a good bird's nest. I'm a bit of a pyromaniac so I love building a good fire. I start with building a platform and pile a bunch of leaves on top of the platform. Then tiny twigs and then slightly larger twigs never getting larger than a cigar. I cast a spark with the sparker into the jute twine and nurse into a nice flame and place it under the leaves. The leaves ignite and we have a good fire.

Practice makes for a great fire on the trail, so learn the basics of fire building. Some make a fire in a log-cabin design, but I use the tee-pee design as it seems to work better for me. You just need to remember to start small and then add larger fuel until you get the size you need.

Step 10
Water Purification

Okay, this subject is usually a source of great debate out there on the trail. Well, for me at least, but I usually like to stir things up a bit –no pun intended.

Bottom line is this: the lightest way to make your water "*drinkable*" is to boil it. Period.

Think about this though… If you are out on the trail, and the only water source is slightly dirty, it will still be "*safe to drink*" if you boil it, but who wants to drink brown water? "S*afe to drink*", or not. For me, this is only an option in a survival situation when I am extremely dehydrated.

Even if you take the pills to treat the water to kill all the little bugs swimming around, it still will not be clear. For me, "drinkable" water is colorless and tasteless, not brown and bug-free. If you are like me, and want your water to be free of the silt, grime, and color, keep reading.

There are a few types of filters on the market right now. You will find pump filters, gravity filters, and squeeze filters. MSR and Katelyn make excellent pump-style filters. I only mention these two brands because I have owned (the MSR Sweetwater) or used both of them on the trail. There are others that are probably just as good, but I don't have personal experience with them, so I don't feel right in recommending them.

Just research the types that are out there and go with the one that makes you most comfortable.

Another lightweight option is the SteriPen. The SteriPen kills bugs with ultraviolet light. Again, I have not used the SteriPen, but I have seen these in use by other backpackers. Again, I do not like the idea of drinking water that has color and taste. However, this *is* a very lightweight option to kill all the microbial critters like Giardia and cryptosporidium. If your water source is a fast running stream, then yes, I can see the Steri-pen a very lightweight and viable option. But not all water sources out in the wilderness are fast running streams.

I personally use the Sawyer Squeeze filter.

I love this filter, not only because it is so light, but because it is good for ONE MILLION GALLONS. Yeah, That's right! A million gallons –if you take care of it.

My 64 ounce bag (approx. 2 liters) and the filter weighs 3 ¾ ounces.

This filter is very easy to use and it will fit onto the bag it comes with, so you can drink directly from the bag. Or if you like, you can filter from the bag into a bottle.

Recently, I was planning for a trip and I needed a replacement cartridge for my Sweetwater pump filter.

A replacement cartridge for the MSR Sweetwater, at the time, cost $45 online, and was rated for 200 Gallons. Well, the Sawyer cost $50 online and is good for a million gallons. Also, my MSR SweetWater weighs 12 1/4oz ounces, so the sawyer rocks it at just over three ounces.

Now I consider myself a fairly intelligent feller, but I don't think it takes a physicist from the Big Bang Theory to figure this one out.

$45 for 200 gallons or $50 for a million gallons. Hmmm….. ya think?

I could pay an additional $5 and get an extra 999,800 gallons. It didn't take me long to make the decision to go with the Sawyer. The only maintenance needed for this filter is to backwash it from time to time, depending on the quality of water you push through it; and Sawyer even provides the syringe that you will use to backwash the filter. I did the math on this filter so check it out:

Let's say that you take one trip a month, and each trip is for seven days. Let's say you drink one gallon of water each day. That is 7 gallons each trip, times 12 trips a year. That is 72 gallons of water each year. 72 gallons of water each year means that the sawyer filter, if you take good care of it, will last almost 14,000 years. The math does not lie:

1,000,000 gallons ÷ 72 gallons each year = 13,888.89 years.

If you take care of it, it could be the last water filter you will ever buy.

At the time of writing this book, the filter was priced for less than $50 at REI.com.

The filter comes with three bags of various sizes and a syringe for backwashing the filter.

---DISCLAIMER---

Now, I feel that I should say something about the products I mention here:

At the time of writing this book I have no affiliation with REI or any other product that I mention herein. nor am I getting any payment or royalties on ANY of the products. I simply believe in giving credit where credit is due.

Step 11
Dual-Purpose Items

Dual-purpose items are essentially items that serve more than one function. They function as designed, and they also can function in other ways, thereby hopefully, eliminating some other item from your pack. Don't compromise your safety, but try to take as many dual-purpose items as possible.

This might be a hard step to take because you will be forced to examine your pack, your gear that you plan on putting into that pack, the clothes on your back and the items in your pockets. Yes, even the items in your pocket can be looked at to see if you can cut some weight. Let's look at some items that might be found in a backpack.

Here are just a few ideas on how to limit your weight by selecting dual-purpose items:

- Duct Tape for first-aid situations, or repair.
- A medium fixed-blade knife instead of two knives.
- Extra socks as a pot gripper, or even gloves.
- Bandannas to filter water, or even a bandage.
- Coffee cup as a measuring device.
- A tent stake to dig a hole instead of a trowel.
- You could take an aluminum water bottle, which is heavier than your standard Nalgene bottle, but the aluminum bottle could replace your cook pot —if all you plan on doing for dinner is boiling

water for your dehydrated food. This is an option I am considering.

I no longer *cook* on the trail; I simply boil water and rehydrate my meals in freezer bags so there is no clean-up at the end of the meal.

Figuring out which items to designate as a dual-purpose item might be an on-going process. On your next trip you might learn that this item or that item can be interchangeable with other items. If so, then you can cull these items in the Three Pile process which I will go over in the next Step.

For now, when planning your next trip, take a look at each item in your arsenal differently. Look at your items and see if you can use it for more than one function. An empty stuff sack stuffed with an extra shirt can be used as a pillow.

Now, empty out your pockets. For your trip, take only the most important keys you can think of. I take my truck key (if I'm the one doing the driving) and that's all. I have a way to get into the house when I return home, so I only need my truck key. If I'm not driving, I only take my house key or no keys at all.

Once we get to the trail-head, my key gets tied to a long length of cordage and stored in the lid of my pack, but that's a secret. Shhhhhhh….. Don't tell anyone.

Instead of my big thick leather wallet, I have a small pocket-wallet that I take. I only carry my driver's license, health insurance card, one credit card, and some cash –the bare essentials.

I don't need pictures, business cards, more than one credit card, yadda yadda yadda… All I need is proof that I can drive, proof I have insurance, some cash for snacks, before and after the trip, and one credit card for emergencies. Nothing more.

Bottom line here is to look at your items and see if you can use them for more than their designed purpose. Now, you may not be able to find a dual-purpose for every item in your pack, but if you can find more than one purpose for just a couple of items, then you are doing better than most. I've said it before and I will say it again... *Every Ounce Counts*.

Well, here you are. You are near the end of the book and about to learn a process that I go through after every trip.

Since you're still reading, I can only assume that you either don't think I am crazy, or you understand the mindset that a Gram Weenie is in when planning for a trip.

I realize that some of the stuff mentioned sounds extreme, but let's face it —you need to be extreme when backpacking. You need to have a lot of stuff to stay warm and comfortable on the trail. If you can accomplish this with a lighter pack, you will be much more relaxed on the trip and not as worn out after the trip.

The final step is the Three Pile process that I go through at the end of each trip. So, let's get started.

Step 12
Three Pile Process

This is the final step, but you might find that you will take this step over and over again. I know I do.

I spend weeks preparing for a trip. If I know I have a trip planned for the last weekend in November, I will start putting my pack together during the first week of November. I will pack and unpack and pack again. Then, I do it again.

My wife goes crazy during this time because I have it all upstairs in the living room so I can pack and unpack and do it again.

This way I know what each item weighs and where each item is located within the pack. Then, during the trip each morning, when we break camp to go to the next stop, all the items go into the pack the same way. Because I practiced this packing and unpacking ritual, I remember where everything goes.

The Three Pile Process comes into play after each trip. Once I return home I take a much needed shower –per my wife's standing order. After the shower I get a good night's sleep. Once I am well rested, I will start to unpack all my gear.

As I unpack, I make three piles of all the gear. This is when I start culling items from my pack, if there are any items that need to be culled. I will spread out my tarp, and I start unpacking. For each item I grab I ask myself one simple easy-to-answer question…

How often did I use this item…?

A lot?
Hardly at all?
Never?

Pile One:

This is where I will pile all the gear that I used a lot – basically multiple times a day. Obviously, I would put my hammock and sleeping bag in this pile even though I only used it once a day. But when I did use this item, I used it for hours at a time while I slept or rested.

I also add to the pile my water filter, cook pot and so on. These are items that I can't possibly survive without, even though I used them only once a day during the trip. Review the five areas I discussed in Step Two.

Other items that would go into this pile are my fire kit, personal kit, knife, hat, gloves. Any item that I touched every day of the trip, several times a day, goes in Pile One. Trekking poles, the pack itself, and even my sunglasses, all go here.

Remember, this pile is where you will put items that were actually used during the trip.

Pile Two:
In this pile I will put all the gear that I seldom used. I usually don't have too many items in this pile anymore, but starting out I would put my plastic trowel in this pile. I would also put uneaten food here because I might have taken 7 trail bars, but only ate 5. So, on the next trip I would take 5 trail bars because I remembered what I put in Pile Two on the previous trip.

After enough trips, you will find that you will be able to plan your food supply so well that by the time you reach the parking lot at the end of a trip, you will have already eaten all the food. I have actually gotten my snack bag down so tight that I have eaten my last candy bar at the truck while we are loading it up to start back home. For me, that is planning right and packing light.

I have a long length of 550 paracord tied up into what I call a donut. To follow the Three Pile process to the letter, many items, like my paracord donut, would end up in this pile because I only used it one day and only once that day. After I go over Pile Three, I will explain what to do with these items.

For now, follow the process to the letter and all will be made clear at the end of this step.

Pile Three:
This pile is for the items that you absolutely did not use at all, at any time during the entire trip. Items like your extra batteries, extra socks, and the game camera.

Okay, let me explain that one. On some trips years ago I would take my game camera because I would hear Bigfoot stomping around in camp, so I started taking the game camera when we would car-camp. This bad little habit fell over into my backpacking trips as well because it only weighed 1 pound 8 1/4 ounces. It ended up in Pile Three and was eventually culled from the pack.

Some other items that may go into this pile are extra bandannas, my DIY wood saw, compact radio, water bag (sometimes I would take extra water bags "just in case") bug spray, sun screen, too many fire starter items, my compass, and even my first-aid kit and multi-tool.

Although I did NOT use my first-aid kit, as little as it was at the time, I still put it in Pile Three because I want to follow this process to the letter. Now, moving on.

At some point, other items that ended up in Pile Three are extra clothes, like my insulation layers. On the trips when the forecast was for very cold weather, we planned on it being even colder up on the mountain, so I would over-pack the thicker items of clothing. I have gotten better and have culled some clothes and/or replaced clothes that are lighter and have less bulk. You might want to go back and review Step Seven. At some point those items ended up in the Pile Three.

I do not put uneaten food in pile three because I kept the food in my food bag and I did hit the food bag every day.

Okay, so now all your items should be in one of the three piles. Good job here. Now, what to do with each pile?

Culling Items

Start with Pile Two and take the items that you seldom used and ask yourself, "did I really need to take this item?" If you answered yes, put that item in pile one.

The length of paracord, for instance, always starts in pile two because I only touched this item a time or two, but I must have it, so I put it in pile one during this part of the process. To follow the rules, however, the donut starts out in Pile Two.

You may have used the plastic trowel only once, but you can use a tent stake to dig a hole if necessary. So put the trowel in pile three, because you are now learning how to look at items within your pack as dual-purpose items.

Do this with every item in pile two. Pick an item and decide if you really must have it. If you do, then put it in pile one. Pick another item and ask the same question and if you don't really need it, put it in pile three. Do this for each item until pile two is gone.

Okay, take all the items in pile one, put them back where they are supposed to go so you can take them on your next trip. And take all the items in pile three and absorb them back into your life at home. Do not plan to take those items again because you already asked yourself if you really needed the items, and you told yourself "No".

If you follow this process to the letter, as I do each trip, on your next trip, you should not have a pile three.

Here's a secret… I always have a pile three after each trip. If after your next trip you still have a pile three, don't be too rough on yourself. It happens to the best of us.

We want to have fun on our trips so we tend to take items with us that are fun but not really needed –which is human nature. But these items take up space and add weight so just decide what you really really really need on a trip. Look back at Step Two to review the list to help with your decision.

Good luck and let me know how your progress is going. I hope you get a lighter pack.

12 Steps To a Lighter Pack

Closing

I hope the twelve steps you just read will help you with reducing the weight of you pack. Think about what you are trying to accomplish here.

We are shaving ounces from our pack, much like a golfer tries to shave strokes off his or her game; if each little tip can help them shave one stroke from their game, they will be closer to the coveted green jacket.

Each ounce we shave from our pack is one-step closer to losing a pound. Think about it this way.

If you shave four ounces from four areas of your pack, that is one pound of weight gone. Every ounce counts and 16 of those ounces add up to be a pound.

As I stated at the beginning of the book, 12 steps times 4 ounces each steps is 48 ounces.

48 ounces ÷ 16 = 3 pounds

I would love to hear from you and how much weight this book helped you shave from your pack so look me up at www.swlowe.com or e-mail me at steve@swlowe.com.

See you on the trail.

About Steve

Steve is currently living in Atlanta, GA with his lovely wife and is Director of Client Services and Technical Writer for a software company, but his real passion is on the other side of the office door –the wilderness.

Steve has been camping for longer than he can remember. He would go camping with his family, at a very young age in a pop-up camper, then with his father, in an old Volkswagen bus. He has travels and camped in RVs as well as tents.

Since then, he has graduated to backpacking with friends in the wilderness. When his job will allow, he hits the trail as often as possible. Over the years, he has researched and tested ways of lightening his pack. This long-time search has turned him into a Gram Weenie and he has become obsessed with obtaining the lightest pack possible.

He has offered some of the obsessive tips to other backpackers and the tips seemed to have been well received.

Check him out at www.swlowe.com

If you would like more information on lightening your load, look for his next book *Plan Right and Pack Light –A Gram Weenie's guide to a lighter pack.*

Appendix A

Use the table below to track what you were able to shave from your pack

Step	Ounces Saved
1	
2	
3	
4	
5	
6	
7	
8	
9	
10	
11	
12	
TOTAL OUNCES SAVED:	
÷ 16	Pounds

I would love to hear how you did. Please e-mail me at steve@swlowe.com

12 Steps To a Lighter Pack

Following is a special excerpt of

Plan Right and Pack Light
A Gram Weenie's guide to a lighter pack

From
Steven Lowe

Introduction

I am what some would call a " Gram Weenie " which means I have been converted to Gram Weenieism. I had to give a name to it, so I call it Gram Weenieism. I define "Gram Weenieism" as: *The methodology or way of thinking to obtain the lightest possible pack for backpacking without sacrificing safety or comfort.* Don't confuse this with being an ultra-light backpacker.

A Gram Weenie is not necessarily an ultra-light backpacker, but I would be willing to bet my favorite hammock that ultra-light backpackers are Gram Weenies. You will see the difference as you read on.

I have been camping for as long as I can remember and even longer than that. The earliest trip I know of (only because my parents like to tell this story... a lot) was when I was about three years old. It was a cold moonless night and we were camping in a pop-up camper. Sometime during the night, there was a knock at the door. My folks heard someone saying: "Open up. I'm feezing. Momma, I'm feezing. I'm feezing"

Yeah, it was me.

It seems that I rolled out the back of the popup and hit the ground. Some may argue that this is what is wrong with me today. Anyhow, I loved to go camping with my family. I didn't care if we camped in a little pop-up, in a Winnebago Camper, or in a tent —as I got older. At some point I remember my father taking me and a friend camping. My father slept in the bus and my friend and I slept in a tent. We were about thirteen or so.

I looked forward to spending the time with my father each time he mentioned us going camping. Every trip I make now, brings back fond memories of when I went camping with my dad back when I was a kid.

Since then, I have graduated to backpacking and camping in the wilderness. Starting out, my fellow backpackers and I had heavy packs and took way too much stuff. We would sleep in our tents, on the cold ground and wake up with so many cricks in our backs we sounded like a breakfast cereal as we emerged from the dome shelter and stretched.

We looked like old men crawling out of the doors of our tents at the crack of dawn. We needed at least an hour to work out the kinks in our backs and necks created from the night before.

I started researching lighter this, and less that and started my trek to Gram Weenieism. Yeah that's a word. Folks in the backpacking world know the term "Gram Weenie". A Gram Weenie is backpacker that is obsessively conscious of every ounce and shaves as much weight as they can without giving up safety, security or pushing their limits. More on this later.

Which brings me to the purpose of this book. I want to take you on a journey. I want to try to explain what a Gram Weenie is and why we think the way that we do. I also will offer some tips that will help you start shaving weight from your pack and maybe convert you to Gram Weenieism.

In a previous book *12 Steps To A Lighter Pack* I have broken some tips down to twelve simple steps to help you shave three or more pounds from your pack.

My hope is that you learn and apply some of these principles and practices to your pack. My hope is that you will join me on the lighter side with a lighter pack –which you will be comfortable in taking onto the trail and confident that you will have all that you will need to live a few days to a week or even more, with the lightest pack you have ever taken with you. Wow, did I just say all that in one sentence? Okay, breathe. It will not be a rough journey. It will be a light one.

The English translation of a quote from Lao Tzu states:
> "The journey of a thousand miles
> begins with a single step"

Before we begin our journey, let's talk about a couple of things. With any pack you must (in my opinion) abide by a couple of rules.

Ch. 1
Two Rules to Understand:
The Rule of Three
The rule of three has been around since the beginning of time. It may not have always been known as the Rule of Three but the rules are true no matter what they are called.

The average person in average situations can survive...

- about three minutes without air.
- about three hours without protection from the elements.
- about three days without water.
- about three weeks without food.

The Five Cs
- Cover
- Container for water
- Cutting tool
- Cordage
- Combustion Device

The "five C" listed above need to be in your pack, even if you are on an innocent day hike where *"nothing could possibly go wrong"*.

A report from the online journal *"Wilderness & Environmental Medicine"* has some interesting statistics involving search-and-rescue operations in national parks. This is just for the national parks. These numbers do not include the areas outside of national parks.

"From 1992 to 2007 there were 78,488 people

involved in 65,439 Search And Rescue incidents. These included 2,659 fatalities, 24,288 injured or sick people, and 13,212 "saves," or saved lives."

I could not possibly know every statistic on each of these incidents, but those numbers might have been reduced, if those folks had the five Cs with them.

Just having the equipment, however, is not enough. Like any equipment in your pack, you need to know how to use it. Test your new compass, the new stove, a knife or even a firesteel. Test from home folks. I preach this on my site, in my blog. If you have not tested your new gear at home, don't take it with you or depend on it for your survival.

Ch. 2
Understanding What a Gram Weenie Is

Prior to my first real backpacking experience, I spent a few years camping with a friend of mine, and we would pack our packs and car-camped. We used our packs because it was easy for us to have everything in a pack that we could haul into camp. We planned to go backpacking eventually, but needed to practice our setup, gear, food, and other techniques. We treated this as testing from home, but in the field. I will get into Testing from home later on.

Keep in mind that our "car-camping" excursions involved primitive camping techniques. We would camp just inside the Chattahoochee National Forest and park the truck. We would still have to carry everything about thirty yards or so it was simply easier to use backpacks. Back then both of our packs were over forty pounds. Looking back I couldn't believe we took some of the things that we took. I mean COME ON! 40 pounds? Really?

I knew we could do better. So we started evaluating our packs, and looking for a lighter way to sleep. We thought about a small one-man tent, a Bivy tent, or anything that was lighter than the 3-man 4-season tent that I carried. We both started looking on-line and stumbled upon a website. It was like the clouds parted and the angles rejoiced. (Imitate your own angelic song here)

The site was dedicated to backpacking while sleeping in hammocks, and a ton of DIY tips and tricks for modifying gear and even making hammocks. Josh and I were hooked on hammock camping. I mean big time. The site is www.hammockforums.net.

I purchased a *Hennessy Expedition Asym* hammock as soon as I could, and thought I was doing better. The hammock slept great once I found my "sweet spot". I explain the sweet spot later on. It was a couple of pounds lighter so I felt like I hit the jackpot. Later on I learned how to make my own hammock and sold the Asym to another backpacking buddy, Mike.

My journey to *Gram Weenieism* started when I bought a book on ultra-lightweight backpacking and doing other research that pointed out the Big Three. If you can get the Big Three down to under ten pounds total, you are getting close to Ultra-light backpacking. I explain the Big Three in Chapter three so keep reading. The journey to Gram Weenieism does not stop with the Big Three. Once you see how you can shave a few ounces from your total weight, you too might become a Gram Weenie. It all started with the phrase – **"*Every Ounce Counts*"**. I weigh everything and I count the ounces of everything I can cull from my pack.

If you can take four areas of your pack, and can shave 4 ounces from each area, you will have shaved 16 ounces from your pack.

16 ounces = 1 pound. Once you develop this type of thinking, you too might become a Gram Weenie.

I will share my tips and some stories that go along with these tips and maybe it will help you to lighten up your pack a little bit. If you slip to the ultra-lightweight side, don't blame me. You are the one who kept reading.

For any type of backpacking, knowing your limitations is crucial. Only you know the level of intensity of terrain you are willing to tackle. You know your friends a lot better than I do, so this is a judgment call where your backpacking partners are concerned.

Having said all that, let's talk about what a Gram Weenie is. Once you know your limitations, you will know where and how to cut weight from your pack and other gear to accomplish crossing over to the lighter side of Gram Weenieism.

The more time you spend at a task, be it your job or any hobby, you spend time learning more efficient ways for performing said task. You strive to be better at it. Be the best. You want to get the job done in the best way you know how. You learn new travel routes to work to cut down on time in traffic. You learn new software at work. You research additional methods for the how to part of your favorite hobby.

The rocky path to Gram Weenieism is no different. If purchasing this book is your first step on that path, I want to take this time to commend you.
Okay, that's enough time.

Printed in Great Britain
by Amazon.co.uk, Ltd.,
Marston Gate.